First English Words

Learn English with Daisy, Ben and Keekee!

HarperCollins Publishers

Westerhill Road
Bishopbriggs
Glasgow
G64 2QT

First edition 2012

Reprint 10 9 8 7 6 5 4 3 2 1

© HarperCollins Publishers 2012

ISBN 978-0-00-743157-1

Collins ® is a registered trademark of
HarperCollins Publishers Limited

www.collinslanguage.com

A catalogue record for this book is available
from the British Library

Printed and bound in China by South China
Printing Co. Ltd

Artwork and design by Q2AMedia

Music and lyrics by Iskra Anguelova

Songs arranged and produced by
www.tomdickanddebbie.com

Additional typesetting by
Davidson Publishing Solutions, Glasgow

For the publisher:

Lucy Cooper   Kerry Ferguson   Elaine Higgleton
Lisa Sutherland

**Content developed and compiled by
Karen Jamieson**

This book includes a CD of songs and vocabulary. The tracks on the CD are:

1. Say the alphabet!
2. Song: I can count!
3. Words: I can count!
4. Song: Colour fun
5. Words: Colour fun
6. Song: Shape search
7. Words: Shape search.
8. Song: My body and face
9. Words: My body and face
10. Song: How I feel
11. Words: How I feel
12. Song: My family at home
13. Words: My family at home
14. Song: Things I do
15. Words: Things I do
16. Song: More things I do
17. Words: More things I do
18. Song: What's it like?
19. Words: What's it like?
20. Song: My day
21. Words: My day
22. Song: Playtime
23. Words: Playtime
24. Song: My classroom
25. Words: My classroom
26. Song: Art time
27. Words: Art time
28. Song: Music time
29. Words: Music time
30. Song: My bedtime
31. Words: My bedtime
32. Song: The fruit stall
33. Words: The fruit stall
34. Song: Supermarket visit
35. Words: Supermarket visit
36. Song: Breakfast time
37. Words: Breakfast time
38. Song: Lunchtime
39. Words: Lunchtime
40. Song: A special dinner
41. Words: A special dinner
42. Song: Baking day
43. Words: Baking day
44. Song: My birthday party
45. Words: My birthday party
46. Song: My pets
47. Words: My pets
48. Song: On the farm
49. Words: On the farm
50. Song: Safari sports day
51. Words: Safari sports day
52. Song: Jungle soccer
53. Words: Jungle soccer
54. Song: In the sea
55. Words: In the sea
56. Song: Rock pool band
57. Words: Rock pool band
58. Song: Bugs and mini-beasts
59. Words: Bugs and mini-beasts
60. Song: The weather
61. Words: The weather
62. Song: Summer clothes
63. Words: Summer clothes
64. Song: Winter clothes
65. Words: Winter clothes
66. Song: My town
67. Words: My town
68. Song: My house and garden
69. Words: My house and garden
70. Song: In the park with grandpa
71. Words: In the park with grandpa
72. Song: Fairytale castle
73. Words: Fairytale castle

Contents

The alphabet

 Aa

 Bb

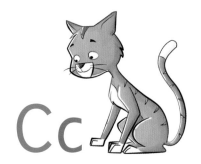 Cc

Dd

Ee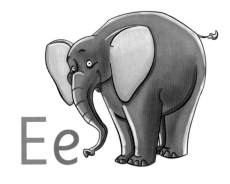

Ff

Gg

Hh

Ii

Jj

Kk

Ll

Mm

Nn

Oo

Pp

Qq

Rr

Ss

Tt

Uu

Vv

Ww

Xx

Yy

Zz

I can count!

1 one

2 two

3 three

4 four

5 five

Activities

1. Can you count to 10?
2. Sing the song!

Song

1, 2, 3, 4, 5
1, 2, 3, 4, 5

6 six

7 seven

8 eight

9 nine

10 ten

I can count, I can count,
I can count to five!

6, 7, 8, 9, 10
6, 7, 8, 9, 10

Can you count? Can you count,
Can you count to ten? YES!

Colour fun

white ——————

blue   green

Activities

1. Find the hidden snake.
2. Sing the song!

Song

Yellow and blue (x4)
make the green of the trees. (x2)

black

purple

red

yellow

orange

Yellow and red (x4)
make the orange of the sun. (x2)

Red and blue (x4)
make the purple of the grapes. (x2)

Shape search

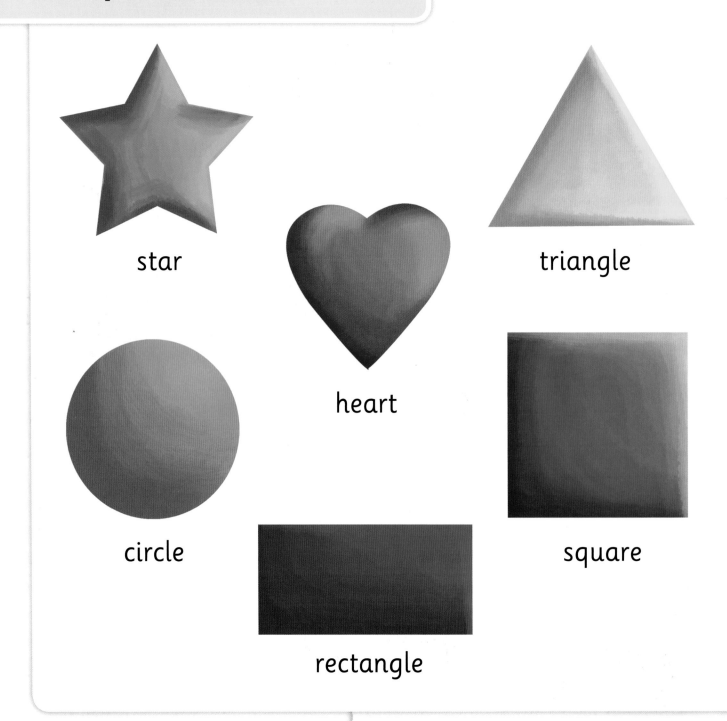

star

heart

triangle

circle

rectangle

square

Activities

1. Find the hidden mouse.
2. Sing the song!

Song

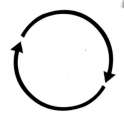 

Round and round the circle goes.
The star shines in the sky.

Count the shapes

Three sides make a triangle.
A heart says 'I love you'.

The square is
like a window.

The rectangle's
like a door. (x2)

My body and face

head

arm

hand

stomach

leg

foot

Activities

1. Find the hidden elephant.
2. Sing the song!

Song

One nose,

One mouth,

hair | nose

eye

ear

mouth

Two eyes,

Two ears. (x 2)

Hair, hair, hair everywhere!

Hair, hair, hair everywhere!

How I feel

angry

sad

happy

tired

Activities

1. Find the hidden apple.
2. Sing the song!

Song

I am hungry. (x 2)
Hamburgers, fries!

hungry

thirsty

scared

shy

I am thirsty. (x 2)
Pour me some milk!

I am happy. (x 2)
Cuddle my cat!

I am tired. (x 2)
Let's go to bed!

My family at home

grandma

grandpa

Activities

1. Find the hidden parrot.
2. Who lives with you?
3. Sing the song!

Song

Look at mummy! Look at daddy!

14

daddy   brother

mummy

me!

sister

There's my sister, baby brother.

Look at grandma! Look at grandpa! Look at me!

This is my family!

Things I do

stand up

sit down

touch my toes

jump

Activities

1. Find the hidden teddy.
2. Sing the song!

Song

Sit down, Daisy,
drink some juice. (x 2)
Sit down Daisy.

eat

drink

cry

laugh

Stand up Ben, and
eat some grapes. (x 2)
Stand up, Ben.

Jump up, high,
then touch your toes. (x 2)
Jump up, Keekee.

Don't cry, Daisy!
Laugh with Ben. (x 2)
Don't cry, Daisy!

More things I do

hold hands

wave

run

walk

Activities

1. Find the hidden shell.
2. Sing the song!

Song

Let's make a circle! (x 2)
All hold hands! (x 2)

clap

turn around

rub my tummy

make a circle

Turn around! (x 2)
Clap your hands! (x 2)

Here is your mummy! (x 2)
Run, run, run! (x 2)

Here is your mummy! (x 2)
Run, run, run! (x 2) Run!

19

What's it like?

slow

fast

small

big

Activities

1. Find the hidden train.
2. Sing the song!

Song

The rabbit is fast and
the turtle is slow.

strong

weak

dirty

clean

The elephant's strong and the baby's weak.

The monkey's small, the gorilla's big!

Dirty hippo! Dirty hippo! Wash it clean!

My day

time to get up

time to get dressed

time for school

playtime

snack time

Song

Good morning! Good morning!
It's time to get up! (x 2)

story time

home time

bath time

bedtime

The school bell is ringing!
It's time for school! (x 2)

The water is lovely!
It's bath time, it's bath time! (x 2)

Good night! Good night!
It's bedtime! It's bedtime! (x 2)

Playtime

plane

ball

puzzle

blocks

Activities

1. Find the hidden duck.
2. What is your favourite toy?
3. Sing the song!

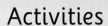

Song

What's in the toy box?
(x 2)

24

toy box

doll

panda bear

train

fire engine

rocket

Doll, panda bear, train.

Rocket and ball, puzzle and plane,

doll, panda bear, train. (x 2)

My classroom

F G H I J
K L M N O
P Q R S T
U V W
X Y Z

teacher

a b c

computer

whiteboard

exercise book

girl

chair

Activities

1. Find the hidden birthday cake.
2. Sing the song!

Song

Girls and boys, girls and boys,

toys

boy

table

books

bag

sit on your chairs!

Open your books! (x 2)

a b c

Look at the teacher,
at the whiteboard! (x 4)

Art time

crayons

glue

scissors

paper

Activities

1. Find the hidden rabbit.
2. Sing the song!

Song

Paper and crayons, markers and brush.
We're painting pictures. This is art class!

marker

pencils

brush

paint

Keekee is drawing. Ben's painting, too.
Daisy is pasting a star with some glue.

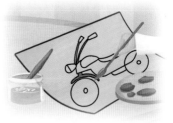

Paper and crayons, markers and brush.
We're painting pictures. This is art time!

Music time

keyboard

triangle

trumpet

drum

Activities

1. Find the hidden pair of scissors.
2. Sing the song!

Song

Let's play music! (x 2)
The violin and xylophone,
the triangle and drum! (x 2)

violin

xylophone

guitar

tambourine

Drum, drum, Keekee,
play the drum!

Daisy plays the
trumpet! Ben - the
tambourine! (x 2)

Drum, drum, Keekee,
play the drum!

My bedtime

1. have a shower

3. put on my
pyjamas

2. dry myself

4. brush my teeth

5. brush my hair

Activities

1. Find the hidden cat.
2. Sing the song!

Song

At the end of the day,
I put on my pyjamas,
brush my teeth, brush my hair.

32

6. go to the toilet

7. wash my hands

8. get into bed

9. cuddle my teddy

10. kiss goodnight

At the end of the day,
I get into bed, cuddle my teddy
and kiss him goodnight.

Kiss my mummy,
say goodnight.
(x 2)

At the end of the day,
I get into bed, cuddle my teddy
and say goodnight!

The fruit stall

watermelons pears strawberries

pineapples oranges

Activities

1. Find the hidden seahorse.
2. What is your favourite fruit?
3. Sing the song!

Song

I like peaches,
I like pears.

grapes

cherries

peaches

apples

bananas

Keekee likes
bananas. (x 2)

Watermelon,
apples, grapes,

oranges and cherries!
(x 2)

Supermarket visit

lettuces

mushrooms

carrots

cucumbers

red peppers

Activities

1. Find the hidden train.
2. Which vegetables do you like best?
3. Sing the song!

Song

Daddy's got a basket. (x 2)

potatoes

broccoli

onions

green peppers

tomatoes

basket

Carrots, lettuce, mushrooms, onions, broccoli.

Daddy's got a basket. (x 2)

Carrots, lettuce, mushrooms, onions, broccoli.

Breakfast time

toast

tea

yoghurt

cup

Activities

1. Find the hidden paintbrush.
2. What do you have for breakfast?
3. Sing the song!

Song

Milk and cereal, bread and jam,
Daisy likes to eat. (x 2)

coffee

cereal

milk

juice

spoon

honey

bread

jam

Mummy, mummy, pass me the honey!
Daddy, daddy, give me the toast!

Milk and cereal, bread and jam,
Daisy likes to eat.

Lunchtime

sushi

chocolate

egg rolls

chicken

tacos

noodles

At school

Activities

1. Find the hidden flower.
2. What's your favourite food?
3. Sing the song!

Song

I am hungry! I am hungry – some pizza, please!

cheese

salad

meat sauce

pizza

corn

pasta

At home

Mummy, pass me, mummy,
pass me, salad and corn!

Noodles, tacos, chicken,
sushi, chocolate and cheese!

I am hungry, I am hungry!
It's time for lunch.

A special dinner

steak

peas

fork

knife

rice

fish

ketchup

Activities

1. Find the hidden flower.
2. Sing the song!

Song

Rice and fish,
steak and peas,

fries

hamburger

soup

baked potato

beans

I'm so hungry, give me some, please! (x 2)

Hamburger, fries, baked potatoes, beans

I'm so hungry, give me some, please! (x 2)

Baking day

butter

syrup

flour

plate

Activities

1. Find the hidden sunglasses.
2. Sing the song!

Song

Mummy's baking cookies.

44

cookies

oven

bowl

sugar

eggs

Daisy's cracking eggs.

Butter, flour, syrup.

This is baking day.

45

My birthday party

ice cream

birthday present

birthday card

Activities

1. Find the hidden bee.
2. Can you count the candles on the cake?
3. Sing the song!

Song

Are you ready for the party? (x 2)

Presents, cards, balloons! (x 3)

46

balloons

popcorn

sandwiches

cake

water

fruit

sweets

Cake and sweets and popcorn, too!

Ice cream, water, fruit! (x 2)

Are you ready for the party? (x 2)

Presents, cards, balloons! (x 3)

My pets

dog

puppy

hamster

guinea-pig

Activities

1. Find the hidden umbrella.
2. Can you hop like a rabbit and stretch like a cat?
3. Sing the song!

Song

Ben and Daisy have some pets:
cat, dog, rabbit. (x 2)

cat

kitten

tortoise

rabbit

Puppy, hamster, guinea pig! (x 2)

Ben and Daisy have some pets:
cat, dog, rabbit!

On the farm

chicken

donkey

goose

duck

Activities

1. Find the hidden octopus.
2. Can you make farm animal noises?
3. Sing the song!

Song

The goose and the duck (x 2) live on the farm, on the farm.

cow

horse

rat

mouse

sheep

The cow and the horse (x 2)
live on the farm as well.

Donkey, chicken,
sheep and mouse
play along with them.

The cow and the horse (x 2)
live on the farm, on the farm.

Safari sports day

crocodile

giraffe

baboon

cheetah

zebra

Activities

1. Find the hidden hat.
2. Sing the song!

Song

The cheetah and the zebra,
the hippo and the rhino.

lion

elephant

rhino

hippo

Run, run, running down
the road! (x 2)

The lion's jumping over the stick!
Jump! Jump! Jump! Jump! (x 2)

Jungle soccer

snake

gorilla

tiger

monkey

chimpanzee

Activities

1. Find the hidden drum.
2. Sing the song!

Song

Jungle soccer is the game

54

parrot

orang-utan

leopard

iguana

gorillas and orang-utans
like to play! (x 2)

Monkeys, tigers
and chimpanzees,

kick the ball and play
with me! (x 2)

55

In the sea

dolphin

shark

seal

octopus

shipwreck

Activities

1. Find the hidden school bag.
2. Sing the song!

Song

In the sea, in the sea
lives a dolphin.

walrus

whale

penguin

turtle

In the sea, in the sea
live his friends.

The octopus, the penguin,
the seal and the turtle,

all live in the sea! (x 2)

Rock pool band

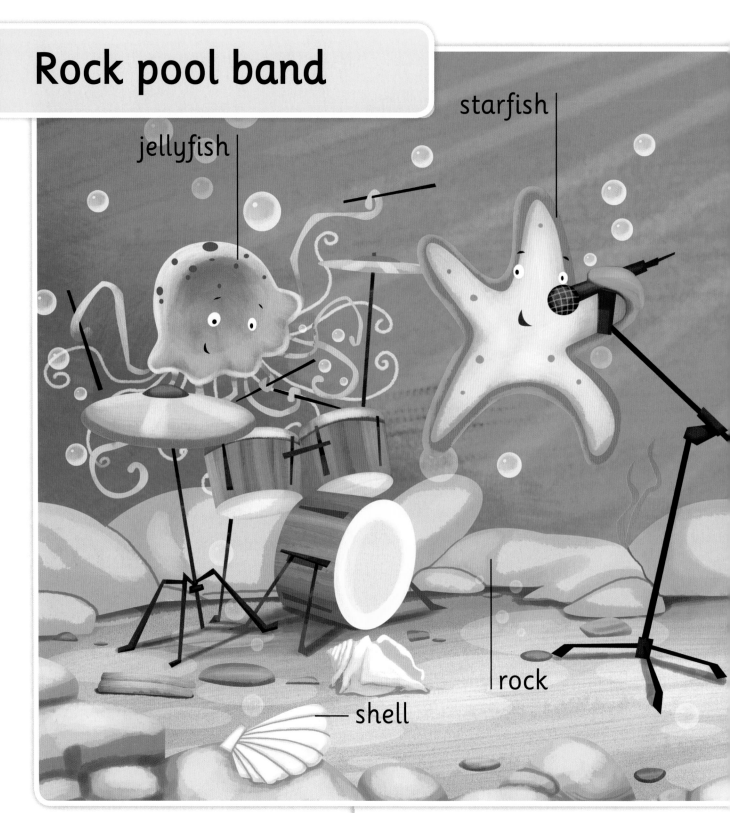

jellyfish

starfish

rock

shell

Activities

1. Find the hidden spoon.
2. Sing the song!

Song

Jellyfish, jellyfish,
play the drums!

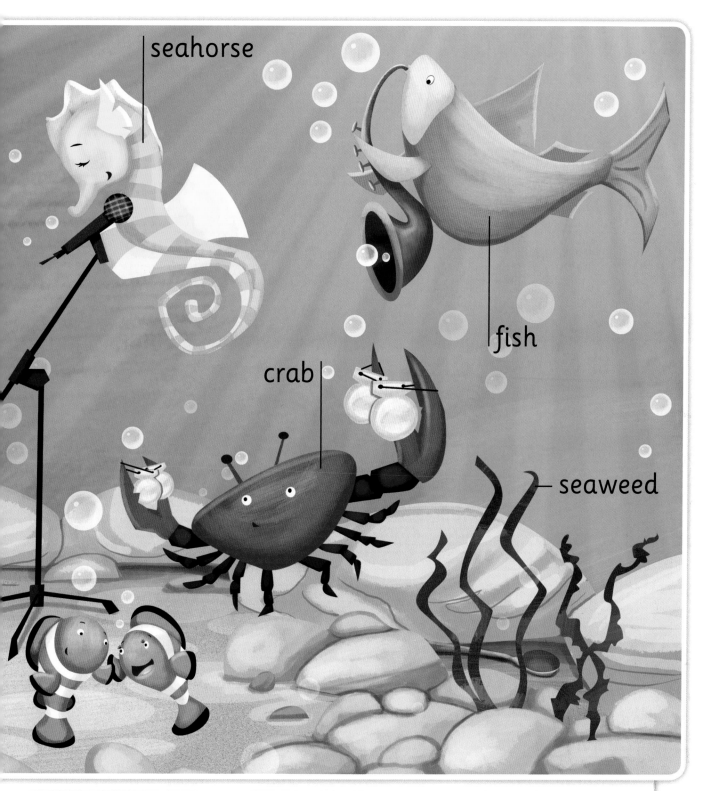

seahorse

fish

crab

seaweed

Starfish, seahorse
sing a song!

Jellyfish, jellyfish,
play the drums!

Seaweed, crab,
join the rock pool band!

Bugs and mini-beasts

butterfly

bee

beetle

ladybird

Activities

1. Find the hidden bananas.
2. Sing the song!

Song

Fly, fly, butterfly,

spider

caterpillar

ant

cricket

come and see your friends! (x 2)

The little bee, the ladybird,
the caterpillar, ant! (x 2)

The weather

rainy

snowy

sunny

windy

62

Activities

1. Find the hidden tiger.
2. Colour a weather picture.
3. Sing the song!

Song

Open the umbrella!
It's rainy, it's rainy!
Open the umbrella!
It's rainy today!

cloudy

hot

cold

stormy

How the snow is falling!
It's snowy, it's snowy!
How the snow is falling!
It's snowy today!

Look the kite is flying!
It's windy, it's windy!
Look the kite is flying!
It's windy today!

How the sun is shining!
It's sunny, it's sunny!
How the sun is shining!
It's sunny today!

Summer clothes

skirt

T-shirt

swimming trunks

swimsuit

Activities

1. Find the hidden trumpet.
2. Sing the song!

Song

Sunglasses, sun hat, sandals and skirt! (x 2)

shirt

sunglasses

sun hat

shorts

dress

sandals

Swimming trunks and swimsuit,
T-shirt and shorts (x 2)

Summer time! Summer time!
Summer time is here! (x 2)

Winter clothes

jacket

trousers

boots

coat

Activities

1. Find the hidden bicycle.
2. Sing the song!

Song

Mummy's wearing boots.

gloves

hat

scarf

sweatshirt

shoes

jeans

Daisy's wearing gloves.

Ben is wearing jeans, shoes and a hat.

Winter time is here!
(x 3)

My town

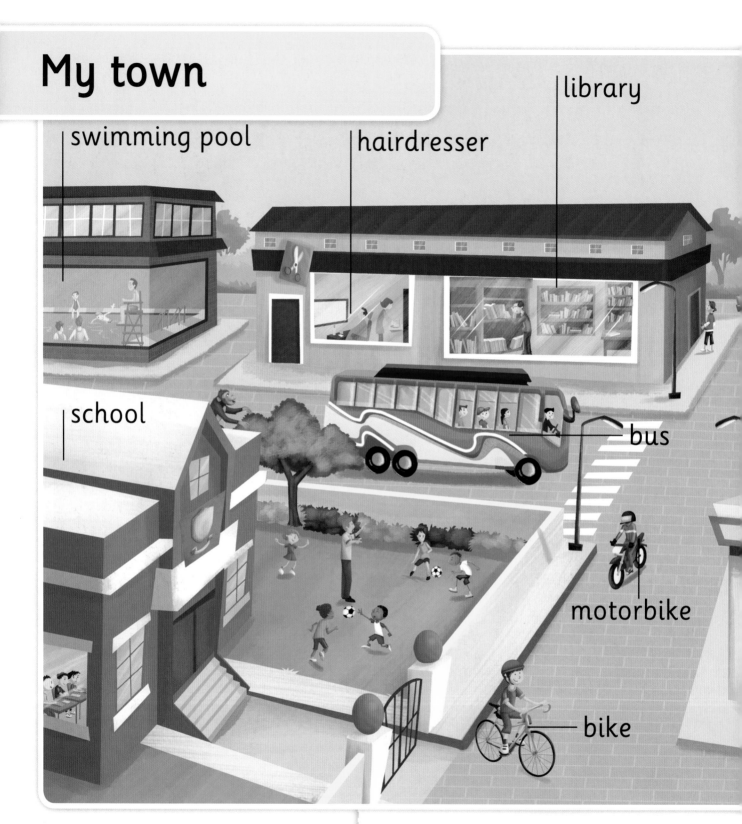

swimming pool

hairdresser

library

school

bus

motorbike

bike

Activities

1. Find the hidden chimpanzee.
2. Which of these things have you seen in your town?
3. Sing the song!

Song

The swimming pool and hairdresser,

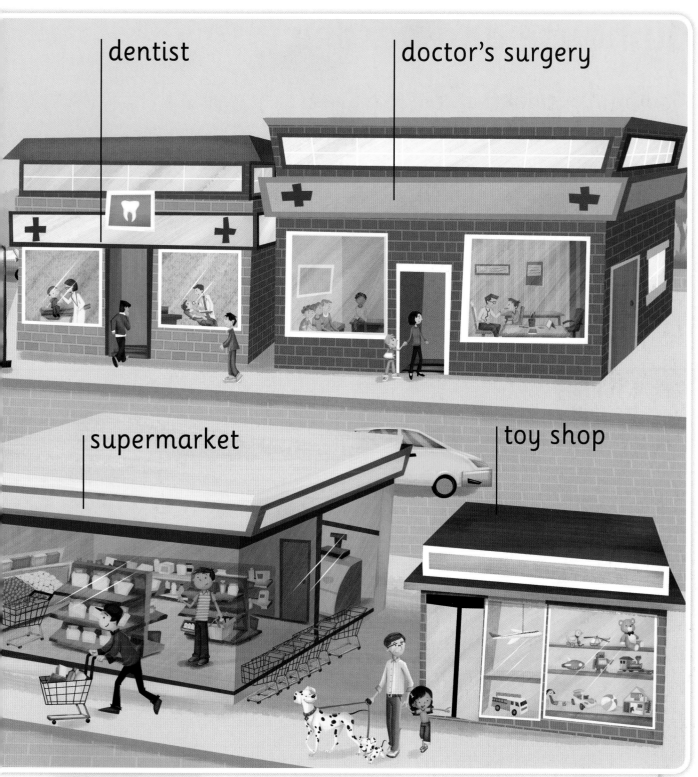

dentist

doctor's surgery

supermarket

toy shop

library and school.
(x 2)

Take the bus!
Ride a bike! (x 2)

To the swimming pool and
hairdresser, library and school.

69

My house and garden

tree

window

flower

garden

Activities

1. Find the hidden guitar.
2. Sing the song!

Song

Open the window!
Close the door! (x 2)

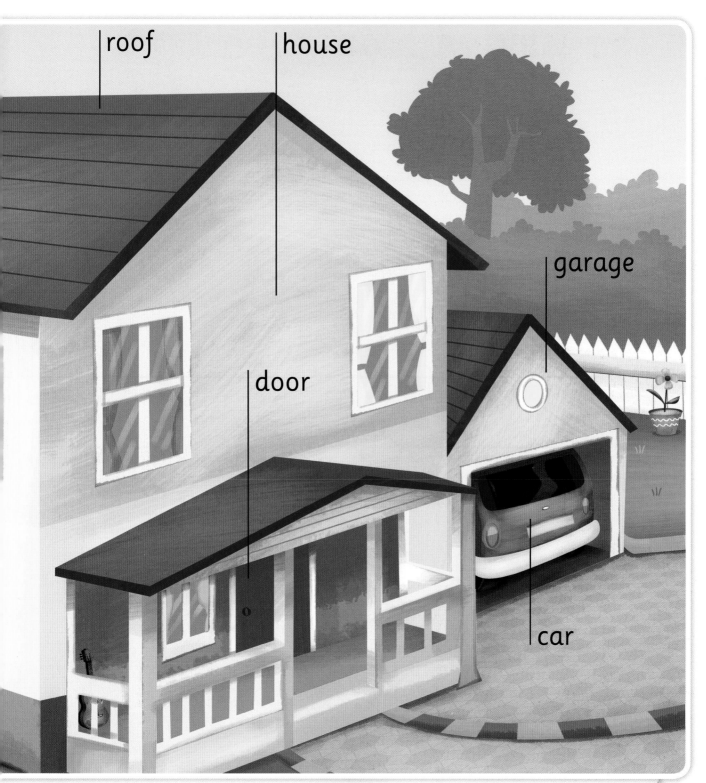

roof

house

garage

door

car

Play in the garden
with the ball! (x 2)

Flowers and trees
around the house. (x 2)

Ben and Daisy run and
play. (x 2)

71

In the park with grandpa

boat

lake

kite

kick scooter

seesaw

Activities

1. Find the hidden tortoise.
2. Sing the song!

Song

Swing, swing,
seesaw, slide!

bird

ball

climbing frame

swing

slide

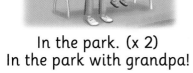

Row a boat,
fly a kite! (x 2)

In the park. (x 2)
In the park with grandpa!

In the park. (x 2)
In the park with grandpa!

Fairytale castle

prince

jester

princess

dragon

Activities

1. Find the hidden crab.
2. Sing the song!

Song

In this castle, oh, so big,

74

castle

knight

minstrel

queen

king

live a princess and
a prince!

Happy minstrels play
a song,

for the king and
the queen!

Index